RUN SALLIE RUN

Run Like Hell Is On Your Heels
The pocket book survival guide for
mature dating women

SARAH BEECHAM POWELL

outskirts
press

Outskirts Press, Inc.
http://www.outskirtspress.com

ISBN: 978-1-4787-8135-6

Outskirts Press and the "OP" logo are trademarks belonging to Outskirts Press, Inc.

This work is dedicated to the processes that help to shape me into who I am. I am Sarah, I am Tina, I am Ms. Beecham, I am Mrs. Powell, I am strong, I am passionate, I am secure, I am hopeful, I am the Lord's own, I am a sojourner, I am loving, I am giving, I am open and, I am expecting something great. I impart this little piece of wisdom in the hope that it will invigorate your spirit and your hope in self. I further dedicate this work to the heroes and loves of my life, Daniel Beecham, Sr. and Eddie D. Powell.

TABLE OF CONTENTS

PREFACE

"Run Sallie Run". You may remember reading a similar sentence in the *Fun with Dick and Jane* books as a child. What was Sallie running from, and why did she feel the need to run? Humorously, this pocket book looks at dating from the perspective of the mature single again woman, and uses song titles and music lyrics to delve into some of the reasons why the author believes that Sallie may have been running. The author was widowed for almost two years after a 32 year marriage when she started this work, and through her dating experiences and various conversations with other mature single women, has come up with several reasons why Sallie may have needed to run like hell from the situations she may have found herself involved in. The topics in the book are meant to evoke laughter, sometimes at yourself, as well as awaken a sense of alertness if you happen to relate to any of the circumstances addressed.

If nothing else, use the book for a conversation piece when you invite your girlfriends over for a cup of coffee or a glass of wine to compare running scenarios. Then compile the information discussed and send it in to runsallierun@yahoo.com for the sequel book. Most of the topics addressed are not in any particular order of importance but randomly cited.

Time to Run Like Hell is on Your Heels When...

THAT FOOL THREW THAT GOOD MAN AWAY—REALLY?

DICK STATES UPON your meeting him that he is going through a divorce. Now ladies, let me state that for the most part, not all men who use that line or who are going through a divorce are culprits. That being said, what woman in her right mind would throw a good man away but a fool? Your common sense and your innate intuition tells you that this sucker is up to no good, was 'throwed' away for being no good, and does not mean you any good; but nooo, you go full speed ahead against every common sense fiber in your body and talk yourself into believing that his pitiful circumstances are anyone else's fault except his own. Why you might ask?—because you are just the type of woman that can correct or fix the things that caused him to go rogue in the first place. Fast forward past the honeymoon stage and all the confusion, heap of lies, and compromising circumstances you have allowed yourself to be exposed to. You will find yourself asking the same question addressed earlier—what woman in her right mind would throw a good man away but a fool?—exactly, nobody but a fool. No real woman worth salt and in her right mind gets rid of a good man. The kind of women that do will be discussed in the next book. For now, we are only dealing with those of us in our right minds. So Sallie you can either run like hell or you can stay; just realize what you are volunteering for and then stop complaining when the girls get together because they are tired of hearing about it.

SARAH BEECHAM POWELL

Slowly Making Me Pay for Things Your Money Should be Handling

———❧———

Have you noticed that things like the paid for trips, dates, dinners, and gasoline have begun to dwindle? On top of that, you have tried to demonstrate that you are not some gold digger by taking on some of the day to day dating expenses; that's exactly what he wanted you to do and was actually pondering what was taking you so long to catch on? You know how it all starts off right? He initially reaches for his billfold to pay for things like quick grocery store visits, gasoline, bites to eat, etc. and insists that you put yours away because 'I got this'. You begin to notice that he doesn't ask you to put that billfold away anymore and slowly starts to let your money pay for things his money was paying for when he was trying to woo you. Then you notice that he has built up the nerve to start asking for small loans which just happen to equal the amount of money spent on the gifts that he has given you. If you are a smart woman you begin to think, don't bother giving me flowers or gifts that you 'borrow' money from me to cover. Sallie, you need to run like hell when you start to pull out your billfold more often than not, loan him money that you don't seem to get back, and when you realize that your bank account decreases whenever you are around him for any length of time. Women are natural nurturers, caregivers, and supporters and you will give of yourself and your resources without hesitation. It's the way we are built. If Dick is not adding to your bank balance or at least contributing by handling his own, Sallie you need to run like hell to keep from spending your money on things his finances should be able to handle. For the sake of self-preservation, realize that his debt is not your debt, nor is his lack of financial resources your problem.

Never Knew Love Like This

DICK TELLS YOU that he has NEVER felt this way about anyone, including all his previous wives, girlfriends, bedmates, buddies, lovers, etc. Why—is it because you are sooo special and a 'Godsend'? In spite of the calls, texts, and voicemails from the list above that you manage to intercept and listen to on his coded cell phone, you still believe that you are 'the one' and are sooo special that he has no need for anyone else now that you have stepped on the scene. Besides, these women just keep seeking after him on their own accord and not of his own doing; he has tried to break away from these relationships but they just won't go away quietly and uneventfully. Why—is it because he is so sought after, or is it that he is doing the seeking? For some unknown irrational reason, you believe that you would be making a huge mistake to give up on a relationship with him and all the associated benefits, which by the way are always in the future tense and rarely make an appearance in the present. You find yourself focusing more on what he says about loving you rather than what he shows. Guess what Sallie, when you allow your intuition and common sense to guide you, it becomes apparent that his actions do not match the words coming out of his mouth. Stop second guessing your own spirit, hoping against the obvious, and making excuses for him.

You need to run like hell when you know full well something is unquestionably wrong with the way his special love makes you feel.

Something, something
Just Ain't Right

No better way to approach this one other than directly. You know your body pretty well. However, for reasons unknown, you ignore the signs that something, something, just ain't right. He tells you that you are the only one he is having *relations* with, yet your body is telling you loudly and clearly that he is lying. Sallie, you believe his lies rather than listen to your own body and intuition. You begin to make up all kinds of stuff in your head like maybe you need to change your detergent or soap. That may be the case, but in your heart of hearts, you know that the signs are there and you need to pay attention to them. What about when you go to the doctor's office often enough that you begin to rotate through several of them so that it will not be noticed that you are asking for the same tests every time you are seen? You know which tests—the ones that check everything from your rooter to your tooter. Sallie, you know the drill by now; if you are allowing yourself to be put through these type of shenanigans in any relationship, and I use that word very loosely, then it's time for you to get to running.

MR. TELEPHONE MAN, THERE'S SOMETHING WRONG WITH MY LINE; YOUR LIES AIN'T WORKING NOW

———— ∿ ————

SALLIE, WHY IS it that when Dick wants to contact you his phone works perfectly fine? He calls and you answer right away. You keep the phone so close to you that it shuts down due to being too hot; you know like phones do when they are left in the heat or direct sunlight too long? When he texts, you not only read them right away, you respond immediately. Since you are so responsive to his contact, you really don't understand why he wouldn't be available or respond to you right away as well. Slowly but surely you begin to notice that a pattern has developed. For instance, he starts responding slower to your contacts after the issue has been addressed or the reset button has been pushed. These little talks or resets start to become more necessary than not. Your calls go unanswered more frequently; he's slower to return those missed calls; his reasons for missing calls or not responding in a reasonable manner just don't make sense; the lies start to actually not work anymore; and then he starts to misplace or leave that phone at home a little too much for anyone with common sense. Sallie, it starts to become clear to you that he is just plain lying and his lies aren't working anymore. Just accept that if a man is truly serious about you and really wants you, he will come looking for you and make it obvious that that's what time it is. You won't have to wonder or be confused about anything. If you are a priority in his life, there's no way you are going to be confused about that.

SARAH BEECHAM POWELL

SUNDAY, MONDAY, TUESDAY, WEDNESDAY, THURSDAY, FRIDAY, SATURDAY LOVE

***

EVER NOTICE THAT on certain days of the week during certain time blocks that you can't reach Dick? You begin to notice that every let's say Thursday something always manages to happen and you aren't able to reach him. You may have been able to talk with him or see him earlier in the day, but after a certain time block he disappears. Why is that you might ask? I'm glad you finally want an answer. Dick has set you up as a part of a rotation schedule. It works a couple of ways. Like tires on a vehicle, Dick rotates his women. The tires on the back of the vehicle do not get as much wear and tear/attention because of their position. The tires on the front of the vehicle tend to experience more activity; new tires are placed on the front and used tires are rotated to the back as a general rule of thumb.

The other way the rotation works is that without your consent you have been assigned certain days within the schedule. The type of women who acquiesce to this type of situation are completely satisfied with the arrangement as long as their prescribed days are not interfered with, nor any normal activity is interrupted that they may be accustomed too. In other words, they are willing and accustomed to man-sharing. You are the newbie and it is expected that eventually you will catch on, cooperate, and play along. Sallie if this type of arrangement is one you don't have a problem with, simply find out what days are assigned to you and roll with it. Otherwise, tell Dick to kick rocks!

Drop That Zero, Get Yourself a Hero

Every Sallie, whether she realizes or acknowledges it, wants a hero in her life. Call it what you want or try and rationalize it away; but ladies, bottom line is that we search for that one man who is able to stand up and act like the idealistic male figure that exists in our minds. Consciously or subconsciously we idolize him whoever he may be. Conflict arises when our real man (zero) does not match up with the idealistic man (hero) in our minds, or doesn't even begin to do those things we envisioned our man would do. What's the difference between Mr. Hero and Mr. Zero other than the h and the z? I'm glad you asked that question. Fix a cup of tea and get comfortable; this may take a little time. Let's start with Mr. Zero because I would like to end this section on a positive note. Mr. Zero puts himself out there like he is what you have been missing in your life. If only he had been in your life earlier, a lot of wasted time and drama could have been avoided. Really? He auditions and, after landing the role of leading man, plays his part extremely well for about 30 days which is really difficult for him. Because he is playing the part of a real man, it is only going to take about 4 to 5 weeks before the real person emerges if you are paying close attention; maybe sooner. You're so busy being wooed (sometimes only in your own mind) that you don't realize that Mr. Zero is doing absolutely nothing above reasonable expectations which include opening doors; being on time for dates-that's if he's actually taking you out and not just showing up eating up your food; and arranging and paying for dates to spend time with you to get to know who you are. This is taking into account that he is actually doing some of these things instead of showing up every time empty-handed as if his presence alone is enough and thankworthy. Mr. Zero not only shows up late and empty-handed, he has the nerve to be hungry and wants something to eat and the audacity to expect to be catered to for his appearance. Furthermore, he comes with the unstated attitude that you must demonstrate your worthiness for his decision to take time out of his schedule just for you.

Mr. Hero, on the other hand, is the exact opposite. You have been dealing with Mr. Zero for so long that you actually forgot that real men do not show up at a

SARAH BEECHAM POWELL

woman's door empty-handed; especially when they are trying to impress or woo her. You give yourself away and let it be known that you have been neglected as soon as you are overly surprised or taken back by simple tangibles that are ordinary for a gentleman such as flowers and wine in hand. When you are dealing with the hero type, certain things are just second nature to him. It's appropriate to show appreciation for these things but you should not be so neglected that they just about knock you off your feet when you do experience them. You stayed in the zero zone way too long—get out as soon as you realize you are there. That's one reason to practice celibacy. If you don't allow Mr. Zero to subliminally convince you to get physical too fast, you will be in better control of your emotions while really examining his patterns, methods, and motives. Back to Mr. Hero. He shows up on time; really wants to get to know who you are; communicates often either via text, phone, email, visits, etc.; spends time with you; keeps his phone off of silence most of the time to actually show what is really going on—this is intentional; comes bearing gifts of some sort-it's the thought that counts; makes real future plans that actually include and benefit you; makes obvious adjustments to his normal routine as you do when something is important to you; when appropriate, puts his money where his mouth is; offers and does things for you that obviously need to be tended to; and makes himself available to you because you are a priority. Sallie if you are in the zero zone you are truly missing out and wasting time, effort, and energy—you need to be running like hell. Drop that zero and get yourself a hero. The difference between zero and hero are as distinct as night and day. What a difference a day makes!!

SARAH BEECHAM POWELL

Almost Doesn't Count

SALLIE EVERYBODY KNOWS almost doesn't count. When you go through your checklist you have tucked away, you know from the start that Dick doesn't even begin to meet the requirements or criteria you previously listed. You convince yourself that your list is outdated, not as important as before, or just simply full of way over the top expectations when you were quite sure of everything you wanted when you initially sat down to compose it. All of a sudden you start to question and even ignore your own desires and begin to settle for what is presented. Wow, take notice of how far you have deviated from your own set standards to accommodate the lack that is in your current special person of interest. Sallie your interest should have immediately started to wane the moment you realized that Dick wasn't even cutting it close to what you wanted for yourself. That checklist should have been taken out and revisited from the beginning. Don't wait until you have crossed 'that' line and gotten emotionally and physically attached and then you remember to look at the list—too late. This is when you start to bend and compromise to make Dick fit when you know he doesn't. Because you have invested yourself, you begin to negotiate with yourself telling yourself that he almost makes the cut, or that if it weren't for this or that he would be just what you wanted. What happens next? *You*, and I stress the word *you*, start to try and fix those things that make Dick an almost kind of guy. You get so involved in making him fit the items on your checklist that you don't realize that you have taken on all of the responsibility to transform him into the man you wanted in your life. If you don't believe me, just pull out your checklist and highlight the area you are currently interested in or helping him to work on. Your desire is to be with a man who is financially stable and independent. Dick's credit is horrible due to a long list of stuff he rambles off when the conversation surfaces. What do you do about this? You determine that he would almost get a checkmark in that area if it were not for blah, blah, blah. You try and help him fix that horrible credit so you can give him that checkmark. This scenario can repeat itself all the way down your whole list. Just realize that almost doesn't count for nothing. Sallie if you have to help Dick meet the requirements on your checklist you need to be running. Remember that your checklist is a composite of what you desire in a stand-up man, not the work you want to put into one to get him to that point. Specifically in the scenario used above, he needs to be financially stable and independent all by himself when he presents himself.

I Think You
Better Call Tyrone

───❧───

Two are better than one. That's what is understood in most relationships, especially when all parties involved are contributing and are being benefited. Sallie when you wake up and discover that you are in a situation where only one of you is benefitting, and most likely it isn't you, it's time for Dick to call Tyrone. Dick has somehow finagled his way into your life, pocketbook, and home without making much of a contribution at all. If you really think about it, all you have gotten on a consistent basis from him is 'dream talk' and futuristic plans with no tangible down payments of any substance, and no manifested evidence to indicate that anything he says is actually going to take place. If you complete a tally, you will discover that you are paying for the gas, food, utilities, rent or mortgage, and even entertainment. Dick might and I mean might put in his measly amount but that's just to throw you off and pretend that he is actually trying to participate. Believe me, he's not; if he were your account balance would reflect that over a period of time. He wants to eat, sleep, recreate, drive, and live as cheaply as he can because he has to try and reserve funds for his extracurricular activities. It costs money to impress new prospects just like it did when he first met you. Dick was putting in overtime and spending money he knew was a limited-time offer; all the while shortening some other Sallie who had been moved down in the order of priority while he was trying to secure you. This is all a part of the rotation strategy. When you realize that Dick is rationing his funds and just riding the Sallie train as long as he can, you need to end that ride and call Tyrone. Tell Tyrone to come and get Dick; come on, come on, come on.

After the Pain

———∞———

WHAT IS ONE of the first things that we as women do when we enter into a new relationship that we swore we wouldn't do? Common sense and experience tell us that we shouldn't, but we do it anyways. That's right, talk about what hurt us in the last relationship thinking that this one will be different and that this person will be more compassionate and understanding. Once we let our guards down, and open up our hearts because of loneliness or just plain boredom and needing something to look forward to, we end up spilling our guts. The more comfortable we become Sallie, the more we spill. A real man who wants a 'realationship' is going to be careful not to cause you any pain by lying, being unfaithful, being deceitful, cheating you out of anything, stressing you, or any of the sort; especially when he has been made aware of the pain you previously endured. Not only does he not want to hurt you, he wishes he could have somehow prevented the things that did. Only a selfish individual like a Dick would compound pain upon pain. A man is a protector; he will protect and shield all that he loves from any hurt, harm, or pain. Sallie, you need to run like hell if you are in a relationship that only compounds your pain instead of relieving and soothing it.

SHE WORKS HARD
FOR THE MONEY

YOU HAVE WORKED hard to get to wherever you are in your station in life. First of all, you graduated from either high school, college, or a training program of some sort. You may have even completed a Master's, Ph.D., or some other professional degree. Over time you have disciplined yourself to purchase only those things that your money can afford and have placed yourself on a budget which you manage most of the times to operate within. As for your credit score, it probably could be improved, but for the most part, it's good enough to handle the things you need it to handle. You may not be able to do all that you desire to do at the moment those things comes to mind, but with a lot of practice in self-deprivation you have found that patience, planning, and payment plans make a lot of goals attainable and achievable for you. You are ever so careful with managing your spending, protecting your credit, and even preparing for that rainy day that it surprises you that you have loosened your grip on money matters and sense when it comes to Dick. In fact, you are totally confused. Allow me to shed some light on the matter. As women, we are natural givers, caregivers, fixers, and nurturers. If something is broke, we are going to fix it. Doesn't matter if it's a man, the car, our children's lives, the finances, whatever. A real woman is a fixer and she will find a way to fix whatever is broken. Now since we know that about ourselves, it is imperative that you understand that boundaries have to be set to determine where the absolute line is to be drawn. What do I mean? You cannot and should not even try to fix what is wrong with Mr. Dick, especially the depressing and disastrous financial hole he has dug for himself for one pitiful reason or another; really doesn't matter. It is simply NOT your responsibility to help him fix his financial messes whatever they are. You didn't help to mess up his finances nor benefit from the spending so why bother? Grown and mature men handle their finances the same way you have and still do as discussed earlier; very carefully and consciously. Why don't we as responsible women exercise good sense in observing Dick's financial behavior long enough to make sense of his spending habits? You may not be paying close attention to his spending habits but you can bet he is observing your money flow. He has observed and knows that you are a responsible type of woman and that you have a backup plan and a rainy day source from which to draw should it become necessary. Remember that you are a natural giver and fixer; you open your dollars and cents to him before you fully realize what is happening. New math: if Dick can't add anything, don't let him take anything; if he didn't bring anything he will leave with the same thing. Sallie, you need to run like hell if you are dealing with a man who has a slew of financial problems and his only solution involves the money and the account that has your name on it.

BAG LADY,
YOU GON HURT YO BACK

THIS PIECE IS very personal. I am in my feelings today and timing is everything. This is a good place and point to end on, and introduce the next book which is *"OUI: Operating under the Influence"*. There's a time in all of our lives that we come to realize that we are carrying things around with us that should have been dumped along the way. Sometimes people have to bring those things to our attention, and other times we realize they are there, but we believe that they are hidden from everyone else—not so. It is apparent by some of the behaviors that we exhibit that we are obviously operating under the influence of some prior experiences. With that said, Sallie, you need to run like hell when Dick shows up putting all the blame on any and everybody who came before you and placing none on himself.

Anytime all the blame is always on someone else and Dick is always the victim, run like hell, fast as hell. He is not even aware of the garbage he is dumping on your back or doesn't give a care because he is comforted and made to feel assured by the idea that he can dump it without taking ownership or responsibility. He has lied to himself so long about who he believes he is that he actually believes that he is held harmless. Of course, you know better. When he shows signs of being extremely jealous, or shall I say hides signs of extreme jealousy, run like hell. When you are constantly confused about the irrational accusations he makes towards you and just about any man you encounter, run like hell, fast as hell. When you find yourself walking and looking down like Ms. Ceily to keep from making eye contact with men for fear he will think you are flirting or being overly open, which means that you are *available*, run like hell because he is crazy as hell. It's not you; it's him every time, all the time. When you begin to feel boxed in and uncomfortable in social settings, because you don't know if it's okay to act like your normal bubbly self, because Dick will get upset and start to act a fool in some embarrassing way or another, it's time. Time for what? I'm glad you asked. It's time to tell Dick to kick rocks. You have prepared yourself, or shall I say life's circumstances have prepared you for a mature and mutually satisfying relationship. Sallie, you don't have the time, nor should you allow your positive energy to be wasted on worthless imagined situations conjured up by some Dick who accuses you of the crap he is either doing himself or he should have been big boy enough to handle when it occurred prior to you. Either way, it's not your garbage to tote around. Dump it right back where it belongs on his back, and run like hell is on your heels.

Hell to the Naw Naw

I'M STILL IN my feelings. I told you this piece was timely and very personal. It ain't over til I say it's over. Sallie life is too short and too full of promise to allow some Dick to taint your time. Learn to enjoy your own life because it's yours. Buy your own roses to smell, buy your own self a gift just for no reason at all other than you can, or because you came to your senses and ran like hell from a situation you know you didn't really want to be involved in in the first place. Stop settling and start demanding, if from no one else at least your own self, the way you want to be treated. Free your mind and the rest will follow. Clearly draw the line and make sure it is not crossed and be ready and quick to serve up the consequences if and when necessary. There are some mature men out there who are looking for mature women who not only know what they want in a man, but also are well aware of who they are or have become. Until these men show up, be prepared to put your running shoes to good use. Sallie, hell to the naw naw to slowing making you pay for things his money should be handling; almost being faithful and being able to be counted on; being put in a rotation schedule; being hooked up with a zero; putting up with pain on top of pain; toting around his old garbage; and being subjected to lies that cover up more lies. If any of these situations exist, it is past time to run like hell is on your heels and you should give yourself permission to experience the power that comes from running from any situation that is not ideal for the betterment of your spirit or emotional and psychological wellbeing.

ACKNOWLEDGEMENTS

I would like to thank all of you who read excerpts and offered chuckles or nods of recognition because something you read resonated with your circumstances or someone you knew. Your agreement, input, and connection with the topics encouraged me to delve openly and deeper with the hope that conversations would ensue. Thank you for your openness to share. Thank you to those who cannot relate as well. It reminds me of a time when these areas were foreign to me as well, but also reminds and informs me that there are those we encounter every day and still we are out of touch with the things they endure and experience; not necessarily a bad thing, it just is. I would also like to acknowledge the special women in my life: my daughters Nelldra Allen, Teresa Beecham, and Sarai Beecham; my sister-cousins Natalie Smith, and Wanda Mack; my mother Nellie Gordon, and my sister-friend of 30 plus years Cherry Chase. These women have added value to my life and nurtured my spirit often.

I reverently acknowledge and thank the most high God who performs all things for me; Psalms 57:2.

Author's Biography

Dr. Sarah Beecham Powell is a native of Montgomery, Alabama. She is a higher education administrator who possesses a natural sense of humor that is prevalent not only in her conversation but also in her writing. She is a gifted orator who uses humor coupled with real life situations to impart practical lessons and information to her readers. Sarah currently resides in Columbus, GA and is newly married to Dr. Eddie D. Powell. She has six children, including one son, Daniel Beecham Jr.; three daughters, Nelldra, Teresa, and Sarai; two stepsons, Marcus and Morgan; and eight grandchildren.

CPSIA information can be obtained at www.ICGtesting.com
Printed in the USA
LVOW08s1030111016

508190LV00001B/1/P